RED FOX

Jen Green

Grolier
an imprint of
■ SCHOLASTIC

www.scholastic.com/librarypublishing

Published 2008 by Grolier
An imprint of Scholastic Library Publishing
Old Sherman Turnpike, Danbury,
Connecticut 06816

For The Brown Reference Group plc
Project Editor: Jolyon Goddard
Copy-editors: Ann Baggaley, Lisa Hughes
Picture Researcher: Clare Newman
Designers: Jeni Child, Lynne Ross,
      Sarah Williams
Managing Editor: Bridget Giles

Volume ISBN-13: 978-0-7172-6282-3
Volume ISBN-10: 0-7172-6282-0

**Library of Congress
Cataloging-in-Publication Data**

Nature's children. Set 3.
    p. cm.
  Includes bibliographical references and
  index.
  ISBN 13: 978-0-7172-8082-7
  ISBN 10: 0-7172-8082-9
  1. Animals--Encyclopedias, Juvenile. I.
  Grolier Educational (Firm)
  QL49.N384 2008
  590.3--dc22
                          2007031568

Printed and bound in China

PICTURE CREDITS

Front Cover: **Nature PL**: Dave Watts.

Back Cover: **Alamy**: Ron Niebrugge, Spirit
Wolf Photography; **Stock Connection
Distribution**; **Shutterstock**: Carolina K.
Smith M. D.

Alamy: Spirit Wolf Photography 30, 33;
Ardea: Ian Beames 29; **FLPA**: W. L. Miller 41;
Nature PL: Laurent Geslin 13, 34; **NHPA**:
Manfred Danegger 5; **Photolibrary.com**:
Daniel Cox 21, Oxford Scientific 38;
Shutterstock: Sam Chadwick 9, Nicola
Gavin 6, Frank Mathers 4; **Still Pictures**:
BIOS/Klein and Hubert 45, BIOS/Pierre
Vernay 17, Patrick Frischknecht 46, Steven
Kazlowski 10, Marilyn Kazmers 22, R. Linke
18, MC Photo 37, 42; **Superstock**: Age
Fotostock 2–3, 14, 26–27.

Contents

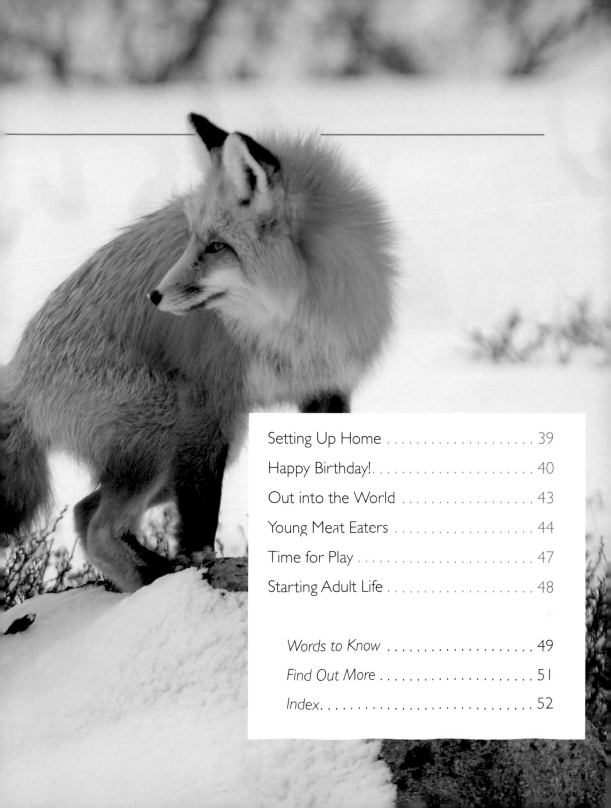

FACT FILE: Red Fox

Class	Mammals (Mammalia)
Order	Carnivores (Carnivora)
Family	Dog family (Canidae); 23 of the 36 species in the dog family are foxes
Genus	*Vulpes* (contains 11 species of foxes)
Species	Red fox (*Vulpes vulpes*)
World distribution	North America, Europe, and Asia, and northern regions of Africa and Central America; now also found in Australia
Habitat	Prefers open country, such as farmland, forest clearings, and tundra
Distinctive physical characteristics	Coat is usually reddish brown with white underside and a bushy, white-tipped tail
Habits	Mainly active at night; live alone when not raising young; both parents care for young
Diet	Mice, voles, rabbits, and other small mammals, birds, eggs, insects, and some plant food

Introduction

The foxes that appear in fables and fairy tales are usually cunning creatures. Many stories describe them as thieves and tricksters—always causing trouble for someone. But are foxes really sneaky and sly?

In real life, foxes have to be clever to find food and to escape their enemies. Rather than being sly, foxes are shy, and wary of people, although they have learned to live near humans. Foxes are intelligent creatures and born survivors. Their flexible habits have enabled them to thrive in many different places.

Like many animals that hunt, a fox's eyes face forward.

In this side view it is easy to see that a red fox is closely related to the dog.

6

Canine Cousins

Red foxes that roam the countryside by night are actually distant cousins of domestic, or pet, dogs. Foxes and dogs are members of a family called canids. This family also includes wolves—which experts have discovered are the ancestors of domestic dogs—coyotes, and jackals.

All canids are meat-eating animals that grab their **prey** using four long, sharp teeth called **canines**. Dogs and foxes also belong to a larger group of animals called carnivores. These animals mainly eat meat. Bears, stoats, weasels, and cats of all sizes are also carnivores.

Fox Family

Foxes are found in most parts of the world. The fox family contains more than 20 **species**, or types, of foxes.

Foxes vary in size. The smallest fox is the fennec fox, from the deserts of North Africa. It weighs just 2.2 pounds (1 kg). It has very large ears that it uses to track prey such as beetles and mice. Animals that survive in the desert have to be tough, and the fennec fox is no exception.

Another hardy survivor is the Arctic fox that lives in the icy far north. This fox's coat changes color with the seasons. In winter the Arctic fox is white, so it blends in with the snowy landscape. In summer, once the snow has melted, its coat changes to a brown color so it can hide among the rocks and grasses.

The white winter fur of an Arctic fox allows it to blend into the snowy background.

9

This red fox has made its home in woodland.

10

At Home Anywhere

The red fox is found in more places than any other fox. In fact, it is one of the world's most widespread **mammals**. Red foxes live in many parts of North America, Europe, and Asia. They can be seen almost everywhere in the northern part of the world, though not in the icy lands of Greenland. They also live as far south as Central America, North Africa, and India. In the mid-19th century humans introduced the red fox to Australia so that it could be hunted for sport. The animals spread and now thrive there, too.

Red foxes dwell in all sorts of country, from bleak, windswept mountains and tundra to woodlands, grasslands, and deserts. They are also at home in places settled by people, such as farms and ranches, and towns and cities, too.

Town and Country

When European settlers arrived in North America, they began to clear the land for farms. Many animals moved farther into the wilderness to keep out of the way of humans, but not red foxes. Fields and pastures fenced off by settlers became the fox's hunting grounds. In winter, these animals took cover from icy winds in the woodlands that provided settlers with timber and fuel. Unlike wolves, foxes seemed to thrive in human company. Soon, they were more common than they had been before the settlers arrived.

Today, it is common to see a red fox roaming through neighborhoods or even city streets. The animals have become completely accustomed to living alongside humans. They often don't wait until sunset to patrol their **territory**, strolling down roads in the middle of the day.

A red fox searches
for tasty morsels
among garbage.

This red fox from Manitoba, Canada, has a thick winter fur coat.

Size and Shape

A full-grown red fox is slim and lightly built, with long, slender legs. The red fox measures 35 to 59 inches (90–150 cm) long. But almost half of this length is made up by the long, bushy tail. That is called a brush. The brush helps the fox to balance as it runs and chases after prey. It is also used as a signal flag to communicate with other foxes.

The male, or **dog**, fox is usually larger than the female, or **vixen**. Red foxes that live in cold northern regions are bigger than their cousins in the south. The extra weight helps the northern foxes keep warm, because big-bodied animals lose heat more slowly than smaller ones.

Snappy Dressers

Red foxes are striking animals. Reddish fur covers the upper part of the body. The chest, belly, tail-tip, and the insides of the large, pointed ears are usually white. The hair on the legs is black, making the fox look as if it is wearing black socks. The thick, bushy tail also has long dark hairs.

Despite their name, not all red foxes are red. Their coat color varies from black, gray, tawny, and rusty red to pale and silvery. Sometimes even **cubs** from the same family have different color coats. Some red foxes have dark hair on their back and shoulders that forms a cross shape. Those are called cross foxes.

Though it looks different, this fox with its dark fur flecked with gray is a red fox.

Its thick coat helps keep this fox warm in winter.

A Warm Coat

The fox's thick fur coat has two layers. Long, smooth hairs called **guard hairs** form the outer layer. They prevent the wind and rain from reaching the underfur, which in turn keeps the fox warm and dry. The soft, fine underfur acts like thermal underwear, trapping warm air next to the fox's skin.

In cold weather, a fox shelters from the wind using trees, rocks, or even a snowbank as a windbreak. It curls up into a ball, and wraps its furry tail over its nose to keep itself warm. In summer, the fox's coat is thinner, so the fox doesn't overheat in the hot weather.

On All Fours

Red foxes are pretty good at both sprinting and long-distance running. These animals can race at a top speed of 30 mph (48 km/h). Equally impressive, they can keep running for hours without getting tired. They can leap high in the air, and also swim well.

Like wolves, foxes have tufts of long hair between the pads of their paws. That helps prevent the fox's feet from freezing as it wades through the snow. If you look closely at a fox's tracks, you can sometimes see marks left by the hairs. Like all members of the dog family, foxes run on their toes.

The ability to jump is just one
of the fox's athletic skills.

As it yawns, this fox shows off its different types of teeth.

Strong Teeth

Foxes need sharp teeth to catch and eat their food. The teeth are covered by a very hard, protective material called enamel. A fox's teeth stay sharp throughout its life. That is because a new layer of enamel grows each year.

Have you ever counted the rings inside a tree stump to see how old the tree was? In a similar way, the rings of enamel on a fox's teeth can be used to tell a fox's age. By counting the rings, scientists have found out that foxes can live to be 12 years old in the wild. However, many foxes are killed by **predators** or disease before they reach this age.

Foxes have teeth of different shapes. As well as the long canine teeth, they also have chisel-like front teeth for nibbling. Their strong back teeth are used for grinding, while jagged **carnassial teeth** easily shear through flesh.

What's for Dinner?

Red foxes will eat almost anything. That's part of the reason they can thrive in so many different places, or habitats. The fox stalks its prey by creeping slowly forward. It then makes a sudden dash to grab its meal. In grasslands, rabbits and hares are the red fox's favorite food. Mice and voles are also common prey, along with snails, beetles, worms, eggs, birds, and even dead animals. City foxes steal food out of garbage cans.

As hunting animals, foxes mainly eat meat. But when food is scarce, they will also eat fruit, including a variety of berries. When food is plentiful and a fox has eaten its fill, it saves the rest for later. It hides its half-eaten kill in a safe place, such as under a rock or beneath the snow.

Expert Trackers

The red fox tracks its prey using its keen senses, including its sensitive nose, sharp eyes, and alert ears. Foxes mainly hunt in darkness, but they might also get hungry during the day.

The twitch of a rabbit hidden in the grass or the scent of a bird nestled in a bush might guide the fox to its meal. A fox can hear the tiny scratching sounds made by a mouse tunneling through the snow. Like a skillful detective, the fox can pick up on the smallest clue.

A fox might watch its prey for a long time without moving a muscle. It then acts with lightning speed. To catch a mouse, a fox pounces like a cat, trapping its small victim in its front paws.

This agile red fox pounces on its unsuspecting prey.

Friend or Foe?

Foxes are unpopular with farmers because they sometimes raid barns and coops to steal hens, turkeys, or eggs. These clever animals are skilled at getting under fences and even opening latches. They are also known to take young lambs.

Despite their snatching of livestock, foxes are also a great help to farmers. They keep down the populations of mice and rats, which break into grain stores and spoil the grain with their droppings. They also catch rabbits, which can harm crops and pasture land by nibbling on the shoots and roots of young plants.

For centuries, foxes have been hunted for sport by packs of dogs and riders on horseback. In many countries that is now against the law. Fortunately, the clever fox is good at outwitting its enemies. It can often outsmart and escape a pack of dogs that has picked up its scent.

Having broken into a hen house, a red fox makes off with one of the farmer's chickens.

A fox patrols its territory.

Keep Out!

Some relatives of foxes, such as wolves, live in packs. A few red foxes live in small family groups, but most are loners, except during the **breeding season**.

Each fox mostly keeps to its own territory— the region where it lives and hunts for food. A lone fox's territory covers between ⅖ to 4 square miles (1–10 sq km). The fox patrols its territory regularly. It leaves urine, droppings, and special scents on the borders. These signals tell other foxes they are not welcome in the territory. Foxes also communicate with other foxes by barking and yelping like dogs, or even howling like wolves.

Fighting Foxes

Some foxes ignore the "keep out" signals left by another fox, and enter its territory. When the two animals meet each other face to face, there might be a fight.

Fighting foxes rear up on their back legs, biting at each other's head and lashing out with their claws. To avoid being badly hurt, the weaker fox usually backs down. Its ears lie back on its head, and it makes a wailing sound. That means, "I give up! You win!"

The winner fluffs up its fur to make itself look bigger. It then struts over to a scent post and leaves its mark. The loser turns tail and flees. It usually escapes with little damage.

When they fight, red foxes are not afraid to use their sharp teeth.

33

A dog red fox
grooms a vixen.

Take Your Partner

Foxes spend much of their time alone. But they pair up for the breeding season. Foxes mate in late winter. That is timed so that the cubs, also called kits or pups, will be born in spring, once milder weather has arrived. The vixen makes a loud, eerie cry, like a scream, to attract her mate.

Sometimes two dog foxes want the same mate. They strut about to impress the female. If neither backs down, they might fight for the chance to mate. The strongest animal wins. The cubs he fathers are likely to be strong and healthy, too.

Foxes often pair for life, teaming up every year to breed. Sometimes the pair is joined by other females. These vixens will not breed, but they will help with rearing the cubs.

A Den for the Young

Shortly before the cubs are born, the fox parents look for a safe home for their young. Where a fox makes its home is called a **den**.

Foxes are not great den diggers. They usually take over the burrow of another animal, such as a badger or a woodchuck. Some vixens make do with a small cave or hollow tree. The fox pair might return to the same den year after year, but they usually have several homes. That way, they can move their cubs if danger threatens.

A fox's den usually has several entrances. One entrance faces south, to catch the sun, which warms the den. Another entrance opens out onto a small clearing. This area will become a playground for the cubs.

A red fox checks for danger before entering its den.

A vixen, curled up in the den, waits for her mate to bring food.

Setting Up Home

The hunting territory of a pair of foxes covers a large area, about the size of 70 city blocks. During the breeding season, this territory is strictly off-limits to other dog foxes. That is because other foxes might harm the cubs.

Just before the cubs are born, the vixen gives up hunting, and retreats to the den. The male is not allowed inside, but he brings grass and leaves for the female to make a cozy nest. He also acts as "breadwinner," bringing back food for his mate. Any food she does not eat now is saved for later. She will be hungry when she is **nursing** her cubs.

Happy Birthday!

The mother fox gives birth about 52 days after mating. The **litter**, or group of young born at one time, might contain anywhere from four to nine cubs. North American vixens usually have larger families than European foxes.

Newborn fox cubs are helpless bundles of brownish-gray fur. They cannot hear, see, or stand up for the first week or so. They huddle up to their mother's warm body, and wriggle over their brothers and sisters. They drink their mother's rich milk. The vixen does not leave her young at this time. While she nurses her cubs in the den, she relies on the father, and sometimes female helpers, to bring her food.

These red fox cubs
are just five days old.

The nose of this red fox cub has not become pointed yet.

Out into the World

At ten days old, the cubs' eyes are open, and their legs are getting stronger. As soon as they are on their feet, the female allows the father inside the den. He gets to know the cubs, and she leaves him in charge while she goes off hunting. But she never strays far from the den. Her babies need to drink her milk regularly in the first weeks of their life.

As the cubs grow, their ears, nose, and legs get longer. At one month old, they leave the den for the first time. They sway on wobbly legs as they get their first glimpse of the outside world. Everything is very strange at first. A leaf spinning by on the wind can easily scare them and send them scampering back to the safety of the den.

Young Meat Eaters

At about one month old, the cubs begin to eat other foods besides their mother's milk. This time is called **weaning**. Like human babies, fox cubs start with soft food. Their sharp but tiny teeth and young stomach aren't yet ready to chew and digest big chunks of meat.

The mother fox prepares the cubs' food by chewing and swallowing meat. When the cubs beg for food, she coughs up the half-digested meal for them. That might not sound very tasty, but it is easy on a cub's stomach. It is also an easy way for the mother to bring food back to the den.

A month-old red
fox cub takes a walk.

These red fox cubs are having fun, but their play-fighting also develops their bodies and skills.

Time for Play

With each passing day, the cubs get stronger and bolder. They venture farther from the den as they get to know the wide world around them. Play-fighting with brothers and sisters helps to strengthen their muscles. They also practice pouncing on toys that their parents bring back for them, such as feathers, bones, and sticks.

It is now time for the cubs to learn the serious business of hunting. The mother and father bring back live prey for them to practice on. They learn to pounce on mice and voles captured by their parents, and they also chase bees and butterflies. At first the cubs are noisy, and careless. But they soon learn that a good hunter is quiet and careful. These lessons will be vital when they start to hunt on their own.

Starting Adult Life

By early fall the cubs are almost full grown. They have become practiced hunters. It is now time for the fox family to split up. The mother and father leave first. They will not meet up again until the following spring, when it is time to mate again. The young foxes leave the den when they are ready to set off on their own.

If winter hunting is good, the cubs might stay together for a while. But usually they split up. Most cubs travel more than 30 miles (50 km) to find an area where they can set up a new territory. That is a dangerous time for the young animals, but they won't be alone for long. At the start of the new year it will be time to find a mate and start a family of their own.

Words to Know

Breeding season   The time when male and female animals come together to produce young.

Canines   Long, sharp teeth used to grab prey.

Carnassial teeth   Jagged back teeth used to slice through flesh.

Cubs   Young foxes, also called kits or pups.

Den   The home of a fox.

Dog   A male fox.

Guard hairs   The outer hairs of a fox's coat.

Litter   All the young born to a mother at one time.

Mammals	Animals that have hair and nurse their young on milk.
Nursing	When a mother feeds her young with milk from her body.
Predators	Animals that hunt other animals for food.
Prey	An animal that is hunted and eaten by another for food.
Species	The scientific word for animals of the same type that breed together.
Territory	Area that an animal or group of animals lives in and defends from other animals of the same kind.
Vixen	A female fox.
Weaning	When a young animal begins to eat solid food and not just drink milk.

Find Out More

Books

Levine, M. *Red Foxes*. Minneapolis, Minnesota: Lerner Publications, 2004.

Shattil, W. and S. J. Tweit. *City Foxes*. Denver, Colorado: Denver Museum of Natural History/Alaska Northwest Books, 1997.

Web sites

Red Fox
www.enchantedlearning.com/subjects/mammals/fox/ Redfoxprintout.shtml
Facts about red foxes with a picture to print and color in.

Red Fox: Wildlife Notebook Series
www.adfg.state.ak.us/pubs/notebook/furbear/redfox.php
Information about red foxes in the wild.

Index